THE WEST RIDING

Unique Photographs of a Bygone Age

collected by John Benson

DALESMAN BOOKS

1978

£1.75

The Dalesman Publishing Company Ltd.
Clapham (via Lancaster), North Yorkshire

First published 1978

© Text, John Benson, 1978

ISBN: 0 85206 434 9

Printed in Great Britain by
Galava Printing Company Ltd., Hallam Road, Nelson, Lancashire

Contents

The cover photographs, both taken in the 1890s, show: Front: The junction of Southgate and Princess Street, Halifax. Back: Two enthusiasts prepare to photograph a keel approaching Sprotborough Mill, near Doncaster.

Bolton Abbey has been a popular beauty spot with generations of West Riding people. As we see here, the stepping stones across the river Wharfe proved as great an attraction to children in the 1890s as they do today.

Introduction and Acknowledgements

THIS collection represents of course only a very small proportion of the photographs taken in the West Riding before the First World War. The selection is necessarily personal although I have tried to include pictures from all areas and to show as many as possible of the numerous activities which went to make up life in Victorian and Edwardian Yorkshire. The vast majority of the photographs have never been published before and it is hoped that the book will be enjoyed by all those who care about Yorkshire's past.

The book could not have been completed without the willing co-operation of many individuals and organisations who both lent me photographs and responded to my requests for information. My thanks are due to the following for allowing me to reproduce the photographs in this book (the figures refer to pages; B=bottom; L=left; R=right; T=top): Barnsley Metropolitan Council, Central Library, 25T, 26B, 27, 73R; Mrs. M. Birch, 50, 51; Bradford Metropolitan District Directorate of Educational Services, Bolling Hall Museum, 23, 65B, Central Library, 7R, 11, 53B, 56T, Keighley Library, 21, 26T; Mrs. J. Brooks, 29B; Calderdale Metropolitan Borough Museums and Art Galleries Service, Shibden Hall Museum, Front Cover, 7L, 8, 12, 17, 42B, 48L, 58, 64, 66, 67, 68L; Mr. R. D. W. Carter, 24, 69, 71; "A Country Camera" by Gordon Winter, 33; Mr. I. Dewhurst, 20, 22T, 30B, 42T, 61; Doncaster Metropolitan Borough Library Service, Central Library, 15, 34, 60, 72, 80; Doncaster Metropolitan Borough Museums and Arts Services, Cusworth Hall Museum, 38, 40, 41, 73L, Doncaster Museum and Art Gallery, Back Cover, 4, 16, 31, 32, 39, 43, 44, 53T, 62, 63; Mr. G. Hall, 9, 14, 22B, 25B, 28T, 37B, 52, 54L; Mr. J. A. Harrison, 13, 28B; Mr. D. Joy, 10, 47; Leeds Metropolitan District Library, Leeds Central Library, 18, 19, 75, 77; Leeds Central Library and Leeds Department of Education, 49; Mr. R. S. Robinson, 6, 45, 57; Rotherham Metropolitan Borough, Libraries Museum and Art Service, Central Library, 30T, 36B, 37T, 54R, Clifton Museum, 29T, 35T, 36T, 55, 56B, 59T; Sheffield Metropolitan Council, Sheffield City Libraries, 46, 70, 74, 78, 79; Wakefield Metropolitan Council, Pontefract Area Library, 48R, 65T; Mr. R. Young, 35B, 59B, 68R.

For information concerning the photographs I am grateful to Mrs. M. Birch, Mr. R. D. W. Carter, Mrs. F. Crowder, Mr. M. J. Dolby, Mr. L. J. Feiweles, Mr. G. Hall, Mr. R. J. Harrison, Mr. M. Hepworth, Mr. J. R. Jebson, Dr. K. Laybourn, Mr. P. B. Littlewood, Dr. R. G. Neville, Mr. W. A. Smith, Ms Jane Springett, Mrs. E. M. Willmott and Mr. R. Young. I am also grateful for the technical assistance of Mr. R. Cowan of "Cameracraft", Mexborough, and of Mr. G. T. Knight of Wolverhampton Polytechnic. Special thanks are due to Mr. Ian Dewhirst, who could not have been more helpful to an unknown correspondent, and to my wife, Clare, who encouraged me at every stage in the preparation of the book.

The West Riding Scene

Above, left: Like other West Riding textile towns Halifax erected fine municipal buildings during the second half of the nineteenth century. The Town Hall, which was designed by Sir Charles Barry, achitect of the Houses of Parliament, was built at a cost of more than £50,000, and was opened by the Prince of Wales in 1863.

Right: Bradford Town Hall was twice as expensive to build as that at Halifax and among its notable features were the statues of 35 English monarchs along the front of the building. They were carved by the London firm of Farmer and Brindley and cost £63 each. This photograph was taken just before the official opening in September 1873 and shows Queen Victoria's statue being raised to occupy a position above the main entrance.

Opposite: Leeds Town Hall, which cost over £120,000 to build, was opened in 1858 by Queen Victoria and Prince Albert because, it was claimed, everybody was "proud of the Town Hall and felt that it was worthy of Royal inauguration".

Town halls were not of course the only monuments to Victorian municipal pride. The impressive main post office at Halifax was designed by Henry Tanner, architect to the local Board of Works, and was opened in 1887. Its site on Commercial Street covered more than a thousand square yards and total building costs came to well over £10,000.

In Wakefield, meanwhile, one street had come to house a number of civic buildings. This photograph of Wood Street, which was taken just before the First World War, shows the clock tower of the Town Hall (opened in 1880), the columns of the West Riding Court House (built 1807-8) and, in the distance, the County Hall which had been opened in 1898.

The new-found importance of West Riding towns and cities as manufacturing, commercial and trading centres was reflected not only in their municipal architecture but also in the ornate buildings and bustling activity of their main streets, as in this picture of Boar Lane, Leeds, which was taken in 1908.

Above: Another view of Leeds, in the days of the horse tram, looking up Briggate and showing part of Duncan Street.

Opposite: Bradford, too, grew rapidly and by the end of the century had become the leading textile town in the West Riding. This view of Darley Street, the axis of the original shopping area, was taken from Kirkgate in about 1891 and conveys an impression of the wide range of retail activity that was carried on in this part of the city.

Crown Street, Halifax, towards the end of the last century. This view is of interest not only for providing an impression of the shops, fashions and transport facilities of the time, but for reminding us of the prevalence of that curse of all nineteenth century pedestrians —horse manure.

In the south of the county the major urban centre was Sheffield which had grown to become the most important steel town of northern England, its population increasing from 46,000 in 1801 to 407,000 a century later. This view along Pinstone Street, between Fargate and the Moor, was probably taken at around the turn of the century.

The population of Huddersfield also increased greatly, rising from 7,000 at the start of the nineteenth century to some 100,000 when this picture was taken about 1905. The photograph was shot from a vantage point on the High Street looking along the central shopping area, New Street, towards John William Street which had been part of the redevelopment designed to accommodate the building of the railway station in 1852.

Another view of the centre of Huddersfield, this time taken from New Street about 1910. On the left of Kirkgate may be seen the "Kirkgate Buildings" while to the right, just out of sight beyond Freeman Hardy and Willis, is the old market place.

Doncaster, too, grew into an important industrial centre following the arrival of the **Great Northern Railway** in 1849 and the decision four years later to transfer the company's locomotive works to the town. But this picture of High Street (part of the Great North Road) in the 1890s shows that Doncaster long retained a country town atmosphere. On the left may be seen the pillars of Doncaster's best known building, the Mansion House, which had been built in 1748 as a residence for the mayor.

Doncaster market place as it was before 1904. On the right is the Corn Exchange which was erected in 1873, while in the background may be seen the parish church of St. George. The church was completed in 1858 to the design of Sir Gilbert Scott and its 170 foot high tower is reputed to be one of the tallest of any parish church in the country.

Another view of the Great North Road as it ran through Doncaster, showing again the extent to which older patterns of behaviour lingered on to the end of the century. A small flock of sheep is being driven to market (see previous picture) past the colonnaded front of the Guildhall, the building which served as Doncaster's police station until it was demolished in 1968.

Indoor markets also became popular in the West Riding during the Victorian and Edwardian years. Halifax Borough Market, for example, was built in 1895 and this picture shows the interior on a quiet afternoon during the early years of the present century.

While the main thoroughfares of Yorkshire towns and cities certainly presented an image of success and prosperity, in the back lanes and side streets the picture could be very different. These three photographs were taken at the beginning of the present century in the Quarry Hill district of Leeds; they might have been taken in almost any West Riding industrial town.

Left: A photograph of—believe it or not—one of Keighley's more fashionable streets, Church Green, during the 1860s. The shops on the left remain little changed to the present day although those on the right were replaced when the road was widened in 1890. The cameraman, who had adopted a roof-top position in New Bridge Street, has obviously attracted the attention of every passer-by in sight.

Opposite: The view from Quebec Bridge, Keighley, in 1898. This area, in the heart of the town's Westgate slum, was the scene of numerous "free fights" and "Irish rows" until the entire area disappeared during the slum clearance of the 1930s.

Another study of Keighley. This winter scene shows the view looking southwards along Skipton Road towards the centre of the town.

The view along Wharf Street, the main road through Sowerby Bridge, in about 1908. Situated at the junction of the Rochdale and the Calder and Hebble Canals, the town grew in the nineteenth century to become an important canal terminus.

Above: Advertising nineteenth century style. This congested hoarding in Sunbridge Road, Bradford, was publicising, among other things, emigration, the comic opera, concerts, a horse fair, race meetings and public sermons. The photograph was taken in 1884 by a Mr Gaskarth from the door of his stationer's shop opposite the hoarding.

Right: Water supply was an urgent problem in the large towns. In some areas the water companies erected standpipes, each one serving perhaps as many as fifteen or twenty houses. The precise date and location of this picture are not known, although it shows a Bradford street (possibly Barkerend Road) sometime during the second half of the nineteenth century.

School Lane, Kirkheaton, on the outskirts of Huddersfield. The church was much rebuilt in the last century and contains in its churchyard the grave of seventeen children (ten of them under fourteen) who were burnt to death in a local mill fire.

A general view of the polluted village of Kirkburton, some five miles from Huddersfield on the road to Wakefield. When this photograph was taken at the end of the last century Kirkburton was known for its collieries, its woollen mills and its corset factories.

In 1821 the hamlet of Brighouse had a population of under 4,000 but by the mid 'eighties it had developed into a prosperous industrial centre with a population of over 8,000. The town's expansion was due both to its location on the river Calder and to the improvement of road and rail facilities during the early part of the century.

Another, and more attractive, picture of Brighouse, taken some twenty years after the above photograph. Briggate was originally a residential area containing some fine buildings such as Hammerton Hall, the home of the architect of Brighouse Parish Church. Towards the end of the century, though, the street became commercialised, housing shops, banks, an hotel and the town's Mechanics' Institute.

A common figure in many West Riding towns and cities before the First World War, the hot-peas seller. This particular street-trader frequented the Westgate district of Keighley during the 1890s.

From a very early age most working-class children, in Yorkshire as elsewhere, sought amusement and excitement outside their cramped homes and backyards. But because there were few parks, playgrounds or even open spaces in the towns, most play took place in the streets. In this picture we see children stopping to drink at the Kendray Street fountain in Barnsley.

These young children were also photographed in Barnsley crawling among the dirt of the Sheffield Road in about 1912. In the background may be seen the Ebenezer Chapel of the New Connexion Methodists which had been built at a cost of more than £5,000 to replace the New Street Chapel.

A typical West Riding pit village before the First World War. When this picture was taken in about 1912 Dodworth had a population of over three thousand yet, like other mining communities in this part of the south Yorkshire coalfield, enjoyed few amenities of any sort.

Askern, once a fashionable resort boasting a spa, was one of the small villages around Doncaster which were transformed almost overnight by the sinking of new deep pits in the early years of the century. In 1911 its population was just 988, a figure which within a decade had leapt to 3,729. some twenty years after the

The view down Rotherham High Street during the second half of the last century. The building jutting out on the right is the painters and decorators, France and Son, while in the distance, along Doncaster Gate, may be seen the town's South Mill.

It would be a great mistake to suppose that the West Riding consisted entirely—or even chiefly—of built-up areas. This view of South Elmsall confirms that even in such heavily industrialised regions as that between Doncaster and Castleford peaceful, rural communities continued to survive.

A peaceful scene at Whiston on the outskirts of Rotherham. The foundation stone of the New Wesleyan chapel was laid in 1865 with the first service being held the following year. Eight years later a public subscription was raised to put the clock in the tower, although the clock never in fact belonged to the chapel and was always maintained by the parish council.

A very early photograph of the famous Haworth parsonage. The mounds of hay have obviously been retouched but the scarcity of graves and the lack of vegetation on the side wall of the house suggest that the picture was taken in the 1840s when both Emily and Charlotte Brontë were still alive.

The south front of the famous medieval parish church of Adwick-le-Street, just four miles from the centre of Doncaster. The picture probably dates from the late 1880s or early 1890s when the tricycle was at the height of its popularity.

Even closer to Doncaster was the village of Cantley whose church also dated back to the thirteenth century. The vicarage, however, had been built no earlier than the beginning of the nineteenth century, although by the 1890s it had clearly matured into a most attractive home.

The homes of the poor were naturally not so comfortable. Here, at Newton between Sprotbrough and Doncaster, two young children pose for the cameraman on the floor of the disused quarry which contained both their home and their garden.

At the other end of the social scale at nearby Cusworth Hall, Lady Isabella Katherine Battie-Wrightson and her staff (chauffeur, handyman, estate steward, lady-in-waiting, butler, housekeeper and assistant, two under-butlers, two gamekeepers, two footmen, two kitchenmaids, four gardeners and five housemaids) prepare to offer afternoon tea to the officers of the King's Own Yorkshire Light Infantry in the autumn of 1911. Cusworth Hall, which was built in 1741, now houses an industrial museum.

33

Work

Right: It is not possible positively to identify the date and place at which this picture was taken. But the glass negative from which it has been reproduced was found in the Clifton Museum, Rotherham, and these men were almost certainly working on a farm in the south of the county towards the end of the last century.

Opposite: Agriculture and its associated trades and industries continued to play a most important part in the economic and social life of the West Riding, indeed of the whole country, before the First World War. This photograph was taken at the Anchorage Farm at Sprotborough in 1894.

Right: Another south Yorkshire agricultural scene which shows how young and old alike were required to help around the farm. These women and children were photographed at Wentworth near Rotherham around the turn of the century.

A popular beauty spot on the river Don, Sprotborough corn mill had been built in the mid eighteenth century to replace an even earlier mill. As the demand for corn-grinding diminished, however, it was also used to power a circular saw. The building was finally demolished in 1931.

Blacksmiths performed a most important rôle in Victorian and Edwardian life. Although this photograph of the Adams brothers outside their smithy in Vicarage Lane, Rotherham, was in fact taken after the First World War, the brothers had been working there since before the turn of the century.

Sewer excavations at Bramley Hill, Rotherham, in January 1914. It is easy now to overlook the extent to which nineteenth and early twentieth century industrial and social developments were dependent upon the efforts of the unskilled labourer.

By the beginning of the present century machinery had begun to supersede some of the more back-breaking of manual tasks. This picture, which dates from just before the First World War, shows a mechanical digger being used in the construction of an extension to the Midland Railway in the northern suburbs of Huddersfield.

Mining and quarrying were very
important in the West Riding
before the First World War.
Sinking a new colliery was an
expensive and time-consuming
operation. Although the date
and place of this photograph
aren't known, it almost certainly
shows work on one of the new
pits which were opened around
Doncaster at the turn of the
century.

A view of part of the limestone quarry at Cadeby, between Mexborough and Sprotborough, in about 1895. This provides an interesting illustration of the laborious way in which the stone was still being won even at this comparatively late date.

Two scenes in the Victoria Mustard Works, Doncaster, c. 1905. The factory had been built on the south bank of the river Don New Cut in 1867 and as well as mustard it produced custard and egg powders, spices, epsom salts "and a wide range of drysaltery goods of every description".
The factory was demolished in 1910 with the building of the North Bridge over the Great Northern Railway.

Half-timers leaving Haggas's Mill at Ingrow, to the south of Keighley, in 1908. The picture was taken at a Saturday lunchtime—which may well explain the cheerful smiles.

This photograph shows a barge passing through a lock near Elland on the Calder and Hebble Navigation. The precise date is not known, although it was probably taken during the 1890s.

A Yorkshire keel under construction at Levitt Hagg on the river Don in about 1900. This type of keel, which measured about 58 feet long by 14 feet wide and had a maximum capacity of about 100 tons, was particularly common on the river Humber and its connecting waterways.

An old boatman at the tiller of a Yorkshire keel on the river Don at Hexthorpe, on the western side of Doncaster, about 1900.

Leeds grew up at the head of the naturally navigable reaches of the river Aire and by the late eighteenth century the Aire and Calder Navigation offered good access to the river Humber. Despite road improvements and the coming of the railways the Aire continued to carry oil inland from Hull and large quantities of coal from the Yorkshire coalfield to the coast.

The Hunter's Bar Toll House on the Sheffield to Chapel-en-le-Frith turnpike road, showing the toll collector leaning against the side of the house. The picture must date from about 1884, the year in which the toll was abolished.

The railway age, as represented by this view of Leeds Wellington station about 1905. The former Midland Railway terminus was rebuilt to form part of Leeds City station in 1938.

47

Above: Local authority employment grew with the expansion of local government services. Here we see the staff of Pontefract Corporation Highways Department (and friends) lined up in front of All Saints Church. In the centre is a steam-driven road roller while on the right is the department's water cart, so essential for the construction and maintenance of the contemporary water-bound roads.

Left: Firemen tackling the Wellington Mills fire at Elland in July 1912. By the end of the nineteenth century most towns had established their own fire-fighting services, although their equipment often remained somewhat rudimentary.

This picture, taken in one of the Leeds board schools which were opened after the 1870 Education Act, shows the emphasis which was placed upon strict discipline and, even in "drill", the mechanical attainment of certain limited skills.

Leisure

The Whitsun celebrations at Oughtibridge parish church, to the north-west of Sheffield, before the First World War when the church still played a most active and important part in everyday life. Sitting to the left of the group assembled on the vicarage lawn (opposite) may be seen Bertie Smith who served as verger for 32 years—only to be succeeded by his wife for another 18 years.

Another Sunday school "Whit walk", this time at Barnsley in 1907.
Whit Monday was also the traditional day for holding many galas,
friendly society processions and other festivals.

The "Sport of Kings" has played a prominent part in Doncaster life for over three and a half centuries; the world famous St. Leger, for example, was first run in 1776. This picture of Doncaster racecourse shows a a race being started during the last decade of the nineteenth century.

Drinking was the most popular recreation in Victorian and Edwardian England and, as might be expected, the West Riding boasted an enormous number of drinking establishments. This pub, the Jolly Butchers Inn on Rawson Street, Bradford, is particularly interesting for the variety of advertisements which it was displaying in 1907.

Left: The Cross Keys Inn in Bread Street, Wakefield, during the First World War. It probably opened as a public house in about 1800 and thirty years later Joseph Metcalf was reported to be brewing there every fortnight. At the end of the street may be seen the tower and spire of Wakefield Cathedral.

Right: This well-known Rotherham pub, the "Old Number 12", was situated at the bottom of College Lane. But like so many other popular nineteenth century drinking places it has now been demolished.

The date and location of this photograph are uncertain. The glass negative, though, was discovered in Rotherham, while the outing was organised by the Plant Hotel in Doncaster which was adjacent to, and named after, the Locomotive and Carriage Works of the Great Northern Railway, popularly known as the "Plant".

The British Temperance Tea and Coffee House at Eldwick Green, near Shipley. The **Bradford Observer** commented in 1884 that since trips to the nearby "Craggs" had become popular, this house had "probably dispensed more ham and eggs and tea than any similar caterer in the neighbourhood".

Rotherham Temperance Society's answer to the pub, the Workman's Coffee and Cocoa House. The Vicar of Rotherham, the Rev. W. Newton, obtained a lease on these premises in Wellgate and the Coffee and Cocoa House was formally opened in November 1877, some three years before this picture was taken in about 1880.

Ice skating was a popular winter recreation in Victorian and Edwardian England and we see here the frozen lake in Roundhay Park, Leeds.
The 616-acre park had been purchased by the city for £139,000 in 1872, at a time when it was still some distance from any built-up area.

Above: The promenade in the People's Park, Halifax, at the beginning of the century. The park, which was laid out by Sir Joseph Paxton, the designer of the Crystal Palace, was given to the town by Sir Francis Crossley, one of a family of Halifax benefactors.

Left: Also popular with the people of Halifax were The Rocks, a large outcrop of millstone grit due south of the People's Park. The Rocks were known locally as "Fourteen Corners" because of the large number of separate shelters which this natural formation offered to courting couples.

A popular Rotherham landmark, Birdcage Lodge in Clifton Park. The lodge, like the park, belonged to the Clifton Estate until both were bought by the corporation in 1891. The lodge was eventually demolished soon after the end of the Second World War.

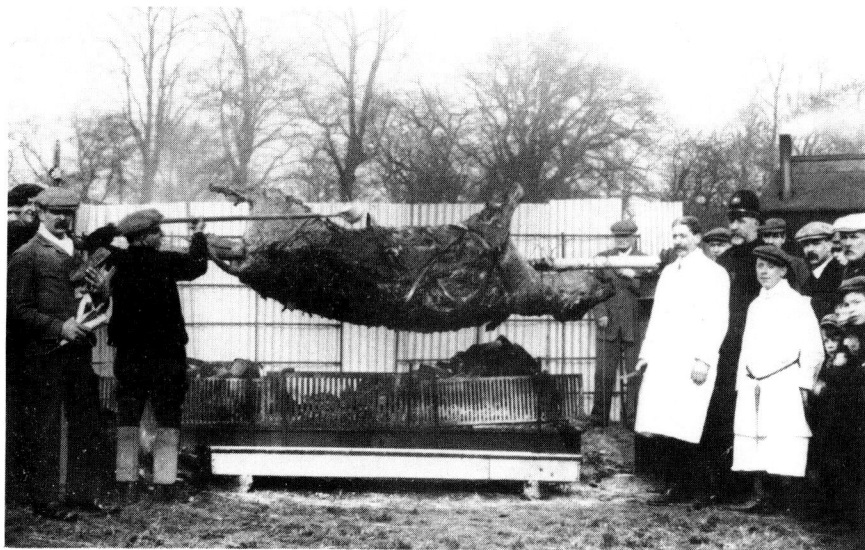

Aristocratic landowners such as the Earls of Harewood and Scarborough were able to exercise enormous power and influence before the First World War. This picture, for example, shows an ox being roasted at Wentworth Woodhouse, near Rotherham, to enable the estate workers of Earl Fitzwilliam to celebrate the christening of his son Peter in 1911.

The opening of the 1910 Hyde Park Horticultural Show, an annual event to raise money for Doncaster Infirmary. The speeches of the Mayor and Mayoress, Councillor and Mrs. Halmshaw, do not appear to be being very well received.

The Doncaster Mutual Co-operative and Industrial Society building decorated for the Royal Agricultural Society's annual show in July 1912. The show, which was held on Doncaster Racecourse, was opened by H.R.H. Prince Arthur of Connaught but was marred by bad weather and by the enforced cancellation of all entries of cattle, sheep and pigs because of an outbreak of foot and mouth disease.

The start of a walking match near Keighley at the Worth Village Gala in the early years of the century, at the height of what was known as "the walking fever".

These photographs from 1904 show some of the activities at a church picnic held at Edlington Wood, a large area of woodland on the western outskirts of Doncaster which was a popular venue for such occasons. In the background to the picture of the cricket match may be seen an early eighteenth century wood-keeper's cottage.

Many parts of the West Riding were visited by entertainers of various kinds. Here the Kew Hill's Travelling Bazaar pose in Elland in 1895 at the top of Coronation Street, the site of the present library.

Nigger minstrels provided another very popular form of entertainment, with every Sunday school, club and institute apparently running its own group. This particular minstrel show was put on at the Northgate Hospital, Pontefract, in 1900.

The opening day of the City of Bradford Exhibition, May 4th, 1904. The exhibition, which was held in the grounds of the newly-opened Cartwright Memorial Hall, was designed to "illustrate, practically, the results achieved by the Textile Industries of the City and district arising from the inventions which have made the name of Edmund Cartwright famous, and combining other branches of industries of a local and general interest".

West Riding — Seven

Many of the larger West Riding towns had thriving entertainment centres. In Halifax, for example, the Victoria Hall, the Palace Theatre and the Theatre Royal were all built at the south end of Commercial Street within a few years at the turn of the century. These pictures of the Victoria Hall show the laying of the foundation stone and the hall as it was when in use.

Left: The visits of national celebrities always provided the opportunity for crowds to gather and meetings to be held. Here General Booth, the founder of the Salvation Army, is received at Elland in 1911, the year before his death.

Above: Royal occasions naturally aroused the greatest interest and enthusiasm. This picture was taken in Rotherham in 1910 and shows part of a thousand-strong procession on its way to All Saints Parish Church for a memorial service to the late King Edward VII.

With the subsequent coronation of King George V the mood changed completely. This "real, living, moving, speaking Union Jack" was created at Bramwall Lane as part of Sheffield's Coronation Pageant.

These two pictures taken in Penistone and Marsden (south-west of Huddersfield) give an idea of the excitement which invariably accompanied any visit to Yorkshire by a member of the royal family. On this occasion in July 1912 King George V (clearly visible in the royal car—opposite) and Queen Mary were making an extended tour across the West Riding.

Motor cycling became popular around the turn of the century and this is the first meeting of the Doncaster Motor Cycle Club in 1910 outside the Woolpack Hotel in the Market Place, Doncaster. The club still exists today as the St. Leger Club.

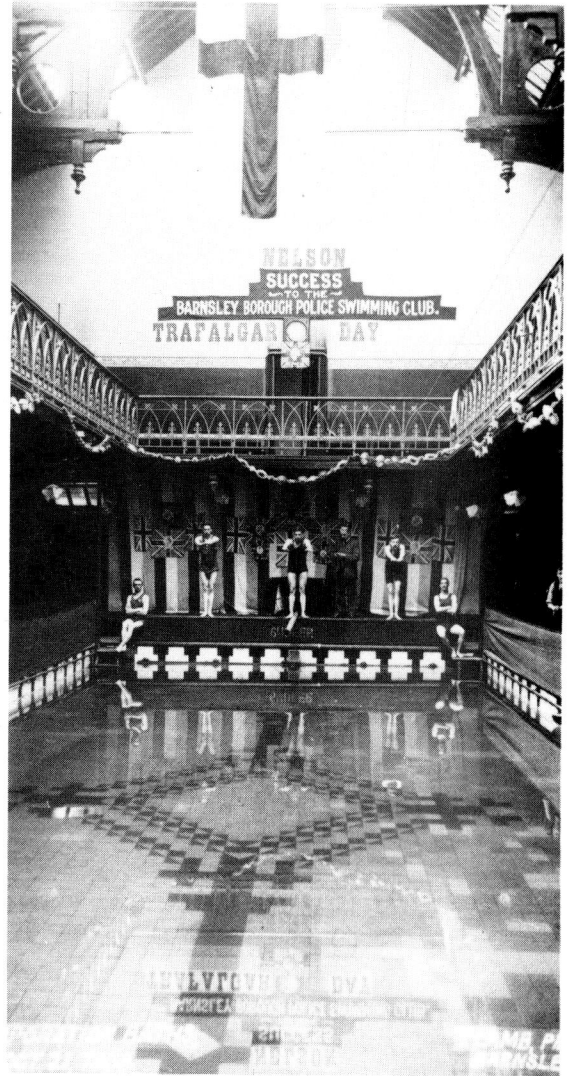

Above: The glass negative of this view of
Blackpool at the turn of the century was
discovered at the Cusworth Hall Museum,
Doncaster. It seems probable therefore that it was
taken by a south Yorkshire visitor to the resort,
taking advantage perhaps of a cheap railway
excursion.

Right: Among the new recreational facilities to be
provided during the second half of the
nineteenth century were local public swimming
pools. In 1846 the government had passed an Act
"for promoting the establishment of Baths and
Wash-Houses for the Labouring Classes" and this
1909 picture shows the Corporation Baths which
opened in York Street, Barnsley, in 1874.

Weddings have always been a time of celebration and family reunion.
We know nothing about the members of this wedding party except that
they were photographed at Barlborough Common (south-east of
Sheffield) in about 1912.

Typical of the middle-class Victorians' desire to mix enjoyment with self-improvement was the Leeds Conversation Club whose members met to discuss all subjects with the exception of politics and religion.
This group waiting at Hellifield station are on the club's 1882 excursion to the Catholic seminary at Stoneyhurst.

Poverty and Death

There was of course a great deal of poverty in Victorian and Edwardian England, much of it treated by the Poor Law authorities by means of admission to the hated workhouse or, more commonly in Yorkshire, by the payment of small sums of "outdoor" relief. The system was administered by locally-elected Boards of Guardians, such as the Dewsbury Board, pictured here during the 1880s.

To avoid the taint of parish relief many of the poor joined friendly societies, insuring against old age, sickness and death. One of the largest was the Ancient Order of Foresters which had been founded in 1790 here at the Old Crown Inn on the south side of Kirkgate in Leeds. When this picture was taken about 1907 the Foresters had nearly a million members in over four and a half thousand branches.

The Poor Law and the friendly societies always found it difficult to combat the vast amount of poverty with which they were confronted. In the exceptional circumstances of a trade depression, a hard winter or a prolonged strike, they found it impossible. These pictures were taken in Sheffield during the Miners' Minimum Wage Strike of 1912 (when over a million miners stopped work) and show the city's poor waiting anxiously to obtain fuel to heat their homes.

A "proper" funeral was the aim of every Victorian and Edwardian.
The poor spent money they could ill afford to ensure that their dead were
"put away respectably" while the funerals of those who had made even
a modest contribution to local life could be most impressive. We see here
preparations being made in 1910 for the funeral of a Doncaster J.P.,
W. J. Huntriss, who had lived in Field House on the Thorne Road.